This planner belongs to

_____

_____

_____

_____

_____

_____

AT A GLANCE

	JANUARY	FEBRUARY	MARCH	APRIL	MAY	JUNE
1	WED	SAT	SUN	WED	FRI	MON
2	THU	SUN	MON	THU	SAT	TUE
3	FRI	MON	TUE	FRI	SUN	WED
4	SAT	TUE	WED	SAT	MON	THU
5	SUN	WED	THU	SUN	TUE	FRI
6	MON	THU	FRI	MON	WED	SAT
7	TUE	FRI	SAT	TUE	THU	SUN
8	WED	SAT	SUN	WED	FRI	MON
9	THU	SUN	MON	THU	SAT	TUE
10	FRI	MON	TUE	FRI	SUN	WED
11	SAT	TUE	WED	SAT	MON	THU
12	SUN	WED	THU	SUN	TUE	FRI
13	MON	THU	FRI	MON	WED	SAT
14	TUE	FRI	SAT	TUE	THU	SUN
15	WED	SAT	SUN	WED	FRI	MON
16	THU	SUN	MON	THU	SAT	TUE
17	FRI	MON	TUE	FRI	SUN	WED
18	SAT	TUE	WED	SAT	MON	THU
19	SUN	WED	THU	SUN	TUE	FRI
20	MON	THU	FRI	MON	WED	SAT
21	TUE	FRI	SAT	TUE	THU	SUN
22	WED	SAT	SUN	WED	FRI	MON
23	THU	SUN	MON	THU	SAT	TUE
24	FRI	MON	TUE	FRI	SUN	WED
25	SAT	TUE	WED	SAT	MON	THU
26	SUN	WED	THU	SUN	TUE	FRI
27	MON	THU	FRI	MON	WED	SAT
28	TUE	FRI	SAT	TUE	THU	SUN
29	WED	SAT	SUN	WED	FRI	MON
30	THU		MON	THU	SAT	TUE
31	FRI		TUE		SUN	

2020

JULY	AUGUST	SEPTEMBER	OCTOBER	NOVEMBER	DECEMBER	
WED	SAT	TUE	THU	SUN	TUE	1
THU	SUN	WED	FRI	MON	WED	2
FRI	MON	THU	SAT	TUE	THU	3
SAT	TUE	FRI	SUN	WED	FRI	4
SUN	WED	SAT	MON	THU	SAT	5
MON	THU	SUN	TUE	FRI	SUN	6
TUE	FRI	MON	WED	SAT	MON	7
WED	SAT	TUE	THU	SUN	TUE	8
THU	SUN	WED	FRI	MON	WED	9
FRI	MON	THU	SAT	TUE	THU	10
SAT	TUE	FRI	SUN	WED	FRI	11
SUN	WED	SAT	MON	THU	SAT	12
MON	THU	SUN	TUE	FRI	SUN	13
TUE	FRI	MON	WED	SAT	MON	14
WED	SAT	TUE	THU	SUN	TUE	15
THU	SUN	WED	FRI	MON	WED	16
FRI	MON	THU	SAT	TUE	THU	17
SAT	TUE	FRI	SUN	WED	FRI	18
SUN	WED	SAT	MON	THU	SAT	19
MON	THU	SUN	TUE	FRI	SUN	20
TUE	FRI	MON	WED	SAT	MON	21
WED	SAT	TUE	THU	SUN	TUE	22
THU	SUN	WED	FRI	MON	WED	23
FRI	MON	THU	SAT	TUE	THU	24
SAT	TUE	FRI	SUN	WED	FRI	25
SUN	WED	SAT	MON	THU	SAT	26
MON	THU	SUN	TUE	FRI	SUN	27
TUE	FRI	MON	WED	SAT	MON	28
WED	SAT	TUE	THU	SUN	TUE	29
THU	SUN	WED	FRI	MON	WED	30
FRI	MON		SAT		THU	31

AT A GLANCE

	JANUARY	FEBRUARY	MARCH	APRIL	MAY	JUNE
1	FRI	MON	MON	THU	SAT	TUE
2	SAT	TUE	TUE	FRI	SUN	WED
3	SUN	WED	WED	SAT	MON	THU
4	MON	THU	THU	SUN	TUE	FRI
5	TUE	FRI	FRI	MON	WED	SAT
6	WED	SAT	SAT	TUE	THU	SUN
7	THU	SUN	SUN	WED	FRI	MON
8	FRI	MON	MON	THU	SAT	TUE
9	SAT	TUE	TUE	FRI	SUN	WED
10	SUN	WED	WED	SAT	MON	THU
11	MON	THU	THU	SUN	TUE	FRI
12	TUE	FRI	FRI	MON	WED	SAT
13	WED	SAT	SAT	TUE	THU	SUN
14	THU	SUN	SUN	WED	FRI	MON
15	FRI	MON	MON	THU	SAT	TUE
16	SAT	TUE	TUE	FRI	SUN	WED
17	SUN	WED	WED	SAT	MON	THU
18	MON	THU	THU	SUN	TUE	FRI
19	TUE	FRI	FRI	MON	WED	SAT
20	WED	SAT	SAT	TUE	THU	SUN
21	THU	SUN	SUN	WED	FRI	MON
22	FRI	MON	MON	THU	SAT	TUE
23	SAT	TUE	TUE	FRI	SUN	WED
24	SUN	WED	WED	SAT	MON	THU
25	MON	THU	THU	SUN	TUE	FRI
26	TUE	FRI	FRI	MON	WED	SAT
27	WED	SAT	SAT	TUE	THU	SUN
28	THU	SUN	SUN	WED	FRI	MON
29	FRI		MON	THU	SAT	TUE
30	SAT		TUE	FRI	SUN	WED
31	SUN		WED		MON	

2021

JULY	AUGUST	SEPTEMBER	OCTOBER	NOVEMBER	DECEMBER	
THU	SUN	WED	FRI	MON	WED	1
FRI	MON	THU	SAT	TUE	THU	2
SAT	TUE	FRI	SUN	WED	FRI	3
SUN	WED	SAT	MON	THU	SAT	4
MON	THU	SUN	TUE	FRI	SUN	5
TUE	FRI	MON	WED	SAT	MON	6
WED	SAT	TUE	THU	SUN	TUE	7
THU	SUN	WED	FRI	MON	WED	8
FRI	MON	THU	SAT	TUE	THU	9
SAT	TUE	FRI	SUN	WED	FRI	10
SUN	WED	SAT	MON	THU	SAT	11
MON	THU	SUN	TUE	FRI	SUN	12
TUE	FRI	MON	WED	SAT	MON	13
WED	SAT	TUE	THU	SUN	TUE	14
THU	SUN	WED	FRI	MON	WED	15
FRI	MON	THU	SAT	TUE	THU	16
SAT	TUE	FRI	SUN	WED	FRI	17
SUN	WED	SAT	MON	THU	SAT	18
MON	THU	SUN	TUE	FRI	SUN	19
TUE	FRI	MON	WED	SAT	MON	20
WED	SAT	TUE	THU	SUN	TUE	21
THU	SUN	WED	FRI	MON	WED	22
FRI	MON	THU	SAT	TUE	THU	23
SAT	TUE	FRI	SUN	WED	FRI	24
SUN	WED	SAT	MON	THU	SAT	25
MON	THU	SUN	TUE	FRI	SUN	26
TUE	FRI	MON	WED	SAT	MON	27
WED	SAT	TUE	THU	SUN	TUE	28
THU	SUN	WED	FRI	MON	WED	29
FRI	MON	THU	SAT	TUE	THU	30
SAT	TUE		SUN		FRI	31

29 MONDAY

30 TUESDAY

1 WEDNESDAY

2 THURSDAY

29 MONDAY	30 TUESDAY	1 WEDNESDAY	2 THURSDAY
7	7	7	7
8	8	8	8
9	9	9	9
10	10	10	10
11	11	11	11
12 PM	12 PM	12 PM	12 PM
1	1	1	1
2	2	2	2
3	3	3	3
4	4	4	4
5	5	5	5
6	6	6	6
7	7	7	7
8	8	8	8
9	9	9	9

3 FRIDAY

4 SATURDAY

5 SUNDAY

3 FRIDAY	4 SATURDAY	5 SUNDAY
7	7	7
8	8	8
9	9	9
10	10	10
11	11	11
12 PM	12 PM	12 PM
1	1	1
2	2	2
3	3	3
4	4	4
5	5	5
6	6	6
7	7	7
8	8	8
9	9	9

Notes

To-Do

- ○
- ○
- ○
- ○
- ○
- ○
- ○
- ○
- ○
- ○
- ○
- ○
- ○
- ○

6 MONDAY	**7** TUESDAY	**8** WEDNESDAY	**9** THURSDAY
7	7	7	7
8	8	8	8
9	9	9	9
10	10	10	10
11	11	11	11
12 PM	12 PM	12 PM	12 PM
1	1	1	1
2	2	2	2
3	3	3	3
4	4	4	4
5	5	5	5
6	6	6	6
7	7	7	7
8	8	8	8
9	9	9	9

7

8

9

10

11

12 PM

1

2

3

4

5

6

7

8

9

Notes

To-Do

○
○
○
○
○
○
○
○
○
○
○
○
○
○

13 MONDAY

7

8

9

10

11

12 PM

1

2

3

4

5

6

7

8

9

14 TUESDAY

7

8

9

10

11

12 PM

1

2

3

4

5

6

7

8

9

15 WEDNESDAY

7

8

9

10

11

12 PM

1

2

3

4

5

6

7

8

9

16 THURSDAY

7

8

9

10

11

12 PM

1

2

3

4

5

6

7

8

9

17 FRIDAY

18 SATURDAY

19 SUNDAY

Notes

17	18	19
7	7	7
8	8	8
9	9	9
10	10	10
11	11	11
12 PM	12 PM	12 PM
1	1	1
2	2	2
3	3	3
4	4	4
5	5	5
6	6	6
7	7	7
8	8	8
9	9	9

to-Do

○
○
○
○
○
○
○
○
○
○
○
○
○
○

20 MONDAY

7

8

9

10

11

12 PM

1

2

3

4

5

6

7

8

9

21 TUESDAY

7

8

9

10

11

12 PM

1

2

3

4

5

6

7

8

9

22 WEDNESDAY

7

8

9

10

11

12 PM

1

2

3

4

5

6

7

8

9

23 THURSDAY

7

8

9

10

11

12 PM

1

2

3

4

5

6

7

8

9

24 FRIDAY

25 SATURDAY

26 SUNDAY

24 FRIDAY	25 SATURDAY	26 SUNDAY
7	7	7
8	8	8
9	9	9
10	10	10
11	11	11
12 PM	12 PM	12 PM
1	1	1
2	2	2
3	3	3
4	4	4
5	5	5
6	6	6
7	7	7
8	8	8
9	9	9

Notes

To-Do

○
○
○
○
○
○
○
○
○
○
○
○
○
○

27 MONDAY | 28 TUESDAY | 29 WEDNESDAY | 30 THURSDAY

27 MONDAY	28 TUESDAY	29 WEDNESDAY	30 THURSDAY
7	7	7	7
8	8	8	8
9	9	9	9
10	10	10	10
11	11	11	11
12 PM	12 PM	12 PM	12 PM
1	1	1	1
2	2	2	2
3	3	3	3
4	4	4	4
5	5	5	5
6	6	6	6
7	7	7	7
8	8	8	8
9	9	9	9

31 FRIDAY　　1 SATURDAY　　2 SUNDAY

31 FRIDAY	1 SATURDAY	2 SUNDAY	Notes
7	7	7	
8	8	8	
9	9	9	
10	10	10	
11	11	11	
12 PM	12 PM	12 PM	
1	1	1	
2	2	2	
3	3	3	To-Do
4	4	4	○
			○
5	5	5	○
			○
6	6	6	○
			○
7	7	7	○
			○
8	8	8	○
			○
9	9	9	○
			○
			○
			○

3 MONDAY

7

8

9

10

11

12 PM

1

2

3

4

5

6

7

8

9

4 TUESDAY

7

8

9

10

11

12 PM

1

2

3

4

5

6

7

8

9

5 WEDNESDAY

7

8

9

10

11

12 PM

1

2

3

4

5

6

7

8

9

6 THURSDAY

7

8

9

10

11

12 PM

1

2

3

4

5

6

7

8

9

7 FRIDAY	8 SATURDAY	9 SUNDAY	Notes
7	7	7	
8	8	8	
9	9	9	
10	10	10	
11	11	11	
12 PM	12 PM	12 PM	
1	1	1	
2	2	2	
3	3	3	To-Do
4	4	4	○
5	5	5	○ ○
6	6	6	○ ○
7	7	7	○ ○
8	8	8	○ ○
9	9	9	○ ○ ○ ○

10 MONDAY	**11** TUESDAY	**12** WEDNESDAY	**13** THURSDAY
7	7	7	7
8	8	8	8
9	9	9	9
10	10	10	10
11	11	11	11
12 PM	12 PM	12 PM	12 PM
1	1	1	1
2	2	2	2
3	3	3	3
4	4	4	4
5	5	5	5
6	6	6	6
7	7	7	7
8	8	8	8
9	9	9	9

14 FRIDAY

15 SATURDAY

16 SUNDAY

14 FRIDAY	15 SATURDAY	16 SUNDAY
7	7	7
8	8	8
9	9	9
10	10	10
11	11	11
12 PM	12 PM	12 PM
1	1	1
2	2	2
3	3	3
4	4	4
5	5	5
6	6	6
7	7	7
8	8	8
9	9	9

Notes

To Do

○
○
○
○
○
○
○
○
○
○
○
○
○
○

17 MONDAY

7

8

9

10

11

12 PM

1

2

3

4

5

6

7

8

9

18 TUESDAY

7

8

9

10

11

12 PM

1

2

3

4

5

6

7

8

9

19 WEDNESDAY

7

8

9

10

11

12 PM

1

2

3

4

5

6

7

8

9

20 THURSDAY

7

8

9

10

11

12 PM

1

2

3

4

5

6

7

8

9

21 FRIDAY

22 SATURDAY

23 SUNDAY

21 FRIDAY	22 SATURDAY	23 SUNDAY
7	7	7
8	8	8
9	9	9
10	10	10
11	11	11
12 PM	12 PM	12 PM
1	1	1
2	2	2
3	3	3
4	4	4
5	5	5
6	6	6
7	7	7
8	8	8
9	9	9

Notes

To-Do

○
○
○
○
○
○
○
○
○
○
○
○
○
○

24 MONDAY   25 TUESDAY   26 WEDNESDAY   27 THURSDAY

24 MONDAY	25 TUESDAY	26 WEDNESDAY	27 THURSDAY
7	7	7	7
8	8	8	8
9	9	9	9
10	10	10	10
11	11	11	11
12 PM	12 PM	12 PM	12 PM
1	1	1	1
2	2	2	2
3	3	3	3
4	4	4	4
5	5	5	5
6	6	6	6
7	7	7	7
8	8	8	8
9	9	9	9

28 FRIDAY

29 SATURDAY

30 SUNDAY

28 FRIDAY	29 SATURDAY	30 SUNDAY
7	7	7
8	8	8
9	9	9
10	10	10
11	11	11
12 PM	12 PM	12 PM
1	1	1
2	2	2
3	3	3
4	4	4
5	5	5
6	6	6
7	7	7
8	8	8
9	9	9

Notes

To-Do

- ○
- ○
- ○
- ○
- ○
- ○
- ○
- ○
- ○
- ○
- ○
- ○
- ○
- ○

31 MONDAY   1 TUESDAY   2 WEDNESDAY   3 THURSDAY

	31 MONDAY	1 TUESDAY	2 WEDNESDAY	3 THURSDAY
7				
8				
9				
10				
11				
12 PM				
1				
2				
3				
4				
5				
6				
7				
8				
9				

4 FRIDAY   5 SATURDAY   6 SUNDAY

4 FRIDAY	5 SATURDAY	6 SUNDAY
7	7	7
8	8	8
9	9	9
10	10	10
11	11	11
12 PM	12 PM	12 PM
1	1	1
2	2	2
3	3	3
4	4	4
5	5	5
6	6	6
7	7	7
8	8	8
9	9	9

Notes

To-Do

- ○
- ○
- ○
- ○
- ○
- ○
- ○
- ○
- ○
- ○
- ○
- ○
- ○
- ○

7 MONDAY

7

8

9

10

11

12 PM

1

2

3

4

5

6

7

8

9

8 TUESDAY

7

8

9

10

11

12 PM

1

2

3

4

5

6

7

8

9

9 WEDNESDAY

7

8

9

10

11

12 PM

1

2

3

4

5

6

7

8

9

10 THURSDAY

7

8

9

10

11

12 PM

1

2

3

4

5

6

7

8

9

11 FRIDAY   **12** SATURDAY   **13** SUNDAY

11 FRIDAY	12 SATURDAY	13 SUNDAY	Notes
7	7	7	
8	8	8	
9	9	9	
10	10	10	
11	11	11	
12 PM	12 PM	12 PM	
1	1	1	
2	2	2	
3	3	3	To-Do
4	4	4	○
5	5	5	○ ○
6	6	6	○ ○
7	7	7	○ ○
8	8	8	○ ○
9	9	9	○ ○ ○ ○

14 MONDAY

7

8

9

10

11

12 PM

1

2

3

4

5

6

7

8

9

15 TUESDAY

7

8

9

10

11

12 PM

1

2

3

4

5

6

7

8

9

16 WEDNESDAY

7

8

9

10

11

12 PM

1

2

3

4

5

6

7

8

9

17 THURSDAY

7

8

9

10

11

12 PM

1

2

3

4

5

6

7

8

9

18 FRIDAY

19 SATURDAY

20 SUNDAY

18 FRIDAY	19 SATURDAY	20 SUNDAY
7	7	7
8	8	8
9	9	9
10	10	10
11	11	11
12 PM	12 PM	12 PM
1	1	1
2	2	2
3	3	3
4	4	4
5	5	5
6	6	6
7	7	7
8	8	8
9	9	9

Notes

To-Do

○
○
○
○
○
○
○
○
○
○
○
○
○
○

21 MONDAY

7

8

9

10

11

12 PM

1

2

3

4

5

6

7

8

9

22 TUESDAY

7

8

9

10

11

12 PM

1

2

3

4

5

6

7

8

9

23 WEDNESDAY

7

8

9

10

11

12 PM

1

2

3

4

5

6

7

8

9

24 THURSDAY

7

8

9

10

11

12 PM

1

2

3

4

5

6

7

8

9

25 FRIDAY

26 SATURDAY

27 SUNDAY

25 FRIDAY	26 SATURDAY	27 SUNDAY
7	7	7
8	8	8
9	9	9
10	10	10
11	11	11
12 PM	12 PM	12 PM
1	1	1
2	2	2
3	3	3
4	4	4
5	5	5
6	6	6
7	7	7
8	8	8
9	9	9

Notes

To Do

- ○
- ○
- ○
- ○
- ○
- ○
- ○
- ○
- ○
- ○
- ○
- ○
- ○
- ○

28 MONDAY

7

8

9

10

11

12 PM

1

2

3

4

5

6

7

8

9

29 TUESDAY

7

8

9

10

11

12 PM

1

2

3

4

5

6

7

8

9

30 WEDNESDAY

7

8

9

10

11

12 PM

1

2

3

4

5

6

7

8

9

1 THURSDAY

7

8

9

10

11

12 PM

1

2

3

4

5

6

7

8

9

2 FRIDAY
3 SATURDAY
4 SUNDAY

Friday 2	Saturday 3	Sunday 4
7	7	7
8	8	8
9	9	9
10	10	10
11	11	11
12 PM	12 PM	12 PM
1	1	1
2	2	2
3	3	3
4	4	4
5	5	5
6	6	6
7	7	7
8	8	8
9	9	9

Notes

To Do

- ○
- ○
- ○
- ○
- ○
- ○
- ○
- ○
- ○
- ○
- ○
- ○
- ○
- ○

5 MONDAY

7

8

9

10

11

12 PM

1

2

3

4

5

6

7

8

9

6 TUESDAY

7

8

9

10

11

12 PM

1

2

3

4

5

6

7

8

9

7 WEDNESDAY

7

8

9

10

11

12 PM

1

2

3

4

5

6

7

8

9

8 THURSDAY

7

8

9

10

11

12 PM

1

2

3

4

5

6

7

8

9

9 FRIDAY

10 SATURDAY

11 SUNDAY

Notes

9	10	11
7	7	7
8	8	8
9	9	9
10	10	10
11	11	11
12 PM	12 PM	12 PM
1	1	1
2	2	2
3	3	3
4	4	4
5	5	5
6	6	6
7	7	7
8	8	8
9	9	9

To-Do

- ○
- ○
- ○
- ○
- ○
- ○
- ○
- ○
- ○
- ○
- ○
- ○
- ○
- ○

12 MONDAY	**13** TUESDAY	**14** WEDNESDAY	**15** THURSDAY
7	7	7	7
8	8	8	8
9	9	9	9
10	10	10	10
11	11	11	11
12 PM	12 PM	12 PM	12 PM
1	1	1	1
2	2	2	2
3	3	3	3
4	4	4	4
5	5	5	5
6	6	6	6
7	7	7	7
8	8	8	8
9	9	9	9

16 FRIDAY

17 SATURDAY

18 SUNDAY

16 FRIDAY	17 SATURDAY	18 SUNDAY
7	7	7
8	8	8
9	9	9
10	10	10
11	11	11
12 PM	12 PM	12 PM
1	1	1
2	2	2
3	3	3
4	4	4
5	5	5
6	6	6
7	7	7
8	8	8
9	9	9

Notes

To-Do

○
○
○
○
○
○
○
○
○
○
○
○
○
○

19 MONDAY 20 TUESDAY 21 WEDNESDAY 22 THURSDAY

19 MONDAY	20 TUESDAY	21 WEDNESDAY	22 THURSDAY
7	7	7	7
8	8	8	8
9	9	9	9
10	10	10	10
11	11	11	11
12 PM	12 PM	12 PM	12 PM
1	1	1	1
2	2	2	2
3	3	3	3
4	4	4	4
5	5	5	5
6	6	6	6
7	7	7	7
8	8	8	8
9	9	9	9

23 FRIDAY | **24** SATURDAY | **25** SUNDAY

23 FRIDAY	24 SATURDAY	25 SUNDAY
7	7	7
8	8	8
9	9	9
10	10	10
11	11	11
12 PM	12 PM	12 PM
1	1	1
2	2	2
3	3	3
4	4	4
5	5	5
6	6	6
7	7	7
8	8	8
9	9	9

Notes

To Do

○
○
○
○
○
○
○
○
○
○
○
○
○
○

26 MONDAY	**27** TUESDAY	**28** WEDNESDAY	**29** THURSDAY
7	7	7	7
8	8	8	8
9	9	9	9
10	10	10	10
11	11	11	11
12 PM	12 PM	12 PM	12 PM
1	1	1	1
2	2	2	2
3	3	3	3
4	4	4	4
5	5	5	5
6	6	6	6
7	7	7	7
8	8	8	8
9	9	9	9

30 FRIDAY

7

8

9

10

11

12 PM

1

2

3

4

5

6

7

8

9

31 SATURDAY

7

8

9

10

11

12 PM

1

2

3

4

5

6

7

8

9

1 SUNDAY

7

8

9

10

11

12 PM

1

2

3

4

5

6

7

8

9

Notes

To-Do

○
○
○
○
○
○
○
○
○
○
○
○
○
○

2 MONDAY

7

8

9

10

11

12 PM

1

2

3

4

5

6

7

8

9

3 TUESDAY

7

8

9

10

11

12 PM

1

2

3

4

5

6

7

8

9

4 WEDNESDAY

7

8

9

10

11

12 PM

1

2

3

4

5

6

7

8

9

5 THURSDAY

7

8

9

10

11

12 PM

1

2

3

4

5

6

7

8

9

6 FRIDAY 7 SATURDAY 8 SUNDAY

6 FRIDAY	7 SATURDAY	8 SUNDAY
7	7	7
8	8	8
9	9	9
10	10	10
11	11	11
12 PM	12 PM	12 PM
1	1	1
2	2	2
3	3	3
4	4	4
5	5	5
6	6	6
7	7	7
8	8	8
9	9	9

Notes

To-Do

○
○
○
○
○
○
○
○
○
○
○
○
○
○

9 MONDAY	**10** TUESDAY	**11** WEDNESDAY	**12** THURSDAY
7	7	7	7
8	8	8	8
9	9	9	9
10	10	10	10
11	11	11	11
12 PM	12 PM	12 PM	12 PM
1	1	1	1
2	2	2	2
3	3	3	3
4	4	4	4
5	5	5	5
6	6	6	6
7	7	7	7
8	8	8	8
9	9	9	9

13 FRIDAY

14 SATURDAY

15 SUNDAY

Notes

13 FRIDAY	14 SATURDAY	15 SUNDAY
7	7	7
8	8	8
9	9	9
10	10	10
11	11	11
12 PM	12 PM	12 PM
1	1	1
2	2	2
3	3	3
4	4	4
5	5	5
6	6	6
7	7	7
8	8	8
9	9	9

To-Do

- ○
- ○
- ○
- ○
- ○
- ○
- ○
- ○
- ○
- ○
- ○
- ○
- ○
- ○

16 MONDAY	**17** TUESDAY	**18** WEDNESDAY	**19** THURSDAY
7	7	7	7
8	8	8	8
9	9	9	9
10	10	10	10
11	11	11	11
12 PM	12 PM	12 PM	12 PM
1	1	1	1
2	2	2	2
3	3	3	3
4	4	4	4
5	5	5	5
6	6	6	6
7	7	7	7
8	8	8	8
9	9	9	9

20 FRIDAY   21 SATURDAY   22 SUNDAY

20 FRIDAY	21 SATURDAY	22 SUNDAY
7	7	7
8	8	8
9	9	9
10	10	10
11	11	11
12 PM	12 PM	12 PM
1	1	1
2	2	2
3	3	3
4	4	4
5	5	5
6	6	6
7	7	7
8	8	8
9	9	9

Notes

To Do

- ○
- ○
- ○
- ○
- ○
- ○
- ○
- ○
- ○
- ○
- ○
- ○
- ○
- ○

23 MONDAY

7

8

9

10

11

12 PM

1

2

3

4

5

6

7

8

9

24 TUESDAY

7

8

9

10

11

12 PM

1

2

3

4

5

6

7

8

9

25 WEDNESDAY

7

8

9

10

11

12 PM

1

2

3

4

5

6

7

8

9

26 THURSDAY

7

8

9

10

11

12 PM

1

2

3

4

5

6

7

8

9

27 FRIDAY   28 SATURDAY   29 SUNDAY

27 FRIDAY	28 SATURDAY	29 SUNDAY	Notes
7	7	7	
8	8	8	
9	9	9	
10	10	10	
11	11	11	
12 PM	12 PM	12 PM	
1	1	1	
2	2	2	
3	3	3	To Do
4	4	4	○
5	5	5	○ ○ ○
6	6	6	○ ○
7	7	7	○ ○
8	8	8	○ ○
9	9	9	○ ○ ○ ○

30 MONDAY   1 TUESDAY   2 WEDNESDAY   3 THURSDAY

30 MONDAY	1 TUESDAY	2 WEDNESDAY	3 THURSDAY
7	7	7	7
8	8	8	8
9	9	9	9
10	10	10	10
11	11	11	11
12 PM	12 PM	12 PM	12 PM
1	1	1	1
2	2	2	2
3	3	3	3
4	4	4	4
5	5	5	5
6	6	6	6
7	7	7	7
8	8	8	8
9	9	9	9

4 FRIDAY	5 SATURDAY	6 SUNDAY	*Notes*
7	7	7	
8	8	8	
9	9	9	
10	10	10	
11	11	11	
12 PM	12 PM	12 PM	
1	1	1	
2	2	2	
3	3	3	*To-Do*
4	4	4	○
			○
5	5	5	○
			○
6	6	6	○
			○
7	7	7	○
			○
8	8	8	○
			○
9	9	9	○
			○
			○
			○

7 MONDAY

7

8

9

10

11

12 PM

1

2

3

4

5

6

7

8

9

8 TUESDAY

7

8

9

10

11

12 PM

1

2

3

4

5

6

7

8

9

9 WEDNESDAY

7

8

9

10

11

12 PM

1

2

3

4

5

6

7

8

9

10 THURSDAY

7

8

9

10

11

12 PM

1

2

3

4

5

6

7

8

9

11 FRIDAY

12 SATURDAY

13 SUNDAY

11 FRIDAY	12 SATURDAY	13 SUNDAY
7	7	7
8	8	8
9	9	9
10	10	10
11	11	11
12 PM	12 PM	12 PM
1	1	1
2	2	2
3	3	3
4	4	4
5	5	5
6	6	6
7	7	7
8	8	8
9	9	9

Notes

To-Do

○
○
○
○
○
○
○
○
○
○
○
○
○
○

14 MONDAY

7

8

9

10

11

12 PM

1

2

3

4

5

6

7

8

9

15 TUESDAY

7

8

9

10

11

12 PM

1

2

3

4

5

6

7

8

9

16 WEDNESDAY

7

8

9

10

11

12 PM

1

2

3

4

5

6

7

8

9

17 THURSDAY

7

8

9

10

11

12 PM

1

2

3

4

5

6

7

8

9

18 FRIDAY

19 SATURDAY

20 SUNDAY

Notes

18 FRIDAY	19 SATURDAY	20 SUNDAY
7	7	7
8	8	8
9	9	9
10	10	10
11	11	11
12 PM	12 PM	12 PM
1	1	1
2	2	2
3	3	3
4	4	4
5	5	5
6	6	6
7	7	7
8	8	8
9	9	9

To-Do

- ○
- ○
- ○
- ○
- ○
- ○
- ○
- ○
- ○
- ○
- ○
- ○
- ○
- ○

21 MONDAY   22 TUESDAY   23 WEDNESDAY   24 THURSDAY

21 MONDAY	22 TUESDAY	23 WEDNESDAY	24 THURSDAY
7	7	7	7
8	8	8	8
9	9	9	9
10	10	10	10
11	11	11	11
12 PM	12 PM	12 PM	12 PM
1	1	1	1
2	2	2	2
3	3	3	3
4	4	4	4
5	5	5	5
6	6	6	6
7	7	7	7
8	8	8	8
9	9	9	9

25 FRIDAY

26 SATURDAY

27 SUNDAY

Notes

25 FRIDAY	26 SATURDAY	27 SUNDAY
7	7	7
8	8	8
9	9	9
10	10	10
11	11	11
12 PM	12 PM	12 PM
1	1	1
2	2	2
3	3	3
4	4	4
5	5	5
6	6	6
7	7	7
8	8	8
9	9	9

To-Do

- ○
- ○
- ○
- ○
- ○
- ○
- ○
- ○
- ○
- ○
- ○
- ○
- ○
- ○

28 MONDAY

7

8

9

10

11

12 PM

1

2

3

4

5

6

7

8

9

29 TUESDAY

7

8

9

10

11

12 PM

1

2

3

4

5

6

7

8

9

30 WEDNESDAY

7

8

9

10

11

12 PM

1

2

3

4

5

6

7

8

9

31 THURSDAY

7

8

9

10

11

12 PM

1

2

3

4

5

6

7

8

9

1 FRIDAY

2 SATURDAY

3 SUNDAY

1 FRIDAY	2 SATURDAY	3 SUNDAY
7	7	7
8	8	8
9	9	9
10	10	10
11	11	11
12 PM	12 PM	12 PM
1	1	1
2	2	2
3	3	3
4	4	4
5	5	5
6	6	6
7	7	7
8	8	8
9	9	9

Notes

To-Do

- ○
- ○
- ○
- ○
- ○
- ○
- ○
- ○
- ○
- ○
- ○
- ○
- ○
- ○

4 MONDAY   # 5 TUESDAY   # 6 WEDNESDAY   # 7 THURSDAY

7	7	7	7
8	8	8	8
9	9	9	9
10	10	10	10
11	11	11	11
12 PM	12 PM	12 PM	12 PM
1	1	1	1
2	2	2	2
3	3	3	3
4	4	4	4
5	5	5	5
6	6	6	6
7	7	7	7
8	8	8	8
9	9	9	9

8 FRIDAY

9 SATURDAY

10 SUNDAY

8 FRIDAY	9 SATURDAY	10 SUNDAY	Notes
7	7	7	
8	8	8	
9	9	9	
10	10	10	
11	11	11	
12 PM	12 PM	12 PM	
1	1	1	
2	2	2	
3	3	3	To-Do
4	4	4	○
			○
5	5	5	○
			○
6	6	6	○
			○
7	7	7	○
			○
8	8	8	○
			○
9	9	9	○
			○
			○
			○

11 MONDAY

| 12 TUESDAY | 13 WEDNESDAY | 14 THURSDAY

7

8

9

10

11

12 PM

1

2

3

4

5

6

7

8

9

15 FRIDAY

7

8

9

10

11

12 PM

1

2

3

4

5

6

7

8

9

16 SATURDAY

7

8

9

10

11

12 PM

1

2

3

4

5

6

7

8

9

17 SUNDAY

7

8

9

10

11

12 PM

1

2

3

4

5

6

7

8

9

Notes

To-Do

○
○
○
○
○
○
○
○
○
○
○
○
○
○
○

18 MONDAY	**19** TUESDAY	**20** WEDNESDAY	**21** THURSDAY
7	7	7	7
8	8	8	8
9	9	9	9
10	10	10	10
11	11	11	11
12 PM	12 PM	12 PM	12 PM
1	1	1	1
2	2	2	2
3	3	3	3
4	4	4	4
5	5	5	5
6	6	6	6
7	7	7	7
8	8	8	8
9	9	9	9

22 FRIDAY

23 SATURDAY

24 SUNDAY

22 FRIDAY	23 SATURDAY	24 SUNDAY
7	7	7
8	8	8
9	9	9
10	10	10
11	11	11
12 PM	12 PM	12 PM
1	1	1
2	2	2
3	3	3
4	4	4
5	5	5
6	6	6
7	7	7
8	8	8
9	9	9

Notes

To-Do

- ○
- ○
- ○
- ○
- ○
- ○
- ○
- ○
- ○
- ○
- ○
- ○
- ○
- ○

25 MONDAY

7

8

9

10

11

12 PM

1

2

3

4

5

6

7

8

9

26 TUESDAY

7

8

9

10

11

12 PM

1

2

3

4

5

6

7

8

9

27 WEDNESDAY

7

8

9

10

11

12 PM

1

2

3

4

5

6

7

8

9

28 THURSDAY

7

8

9

10

11

12 PM

1

2

3

4

5

6

7

8

9

29 FRIDAY

30 SATURDAY

31 SUNDAY

Notes

29 FRIDAY	30 SATURDAY	31 SUNDAY
7	7	7
8	8	8
9	9	9
10	10	10
11	11	11
12 PM	12 PM	12 PM
1	1	1
2	2	2
3	3	3
4	4	4
5	5	5
6	6	6
7	7	7
8	8	8
9	9	9

To-Do

○
○
○
○
○
○
○
○
○
○
○
○
○
○

1 MONDAY   2 TUESDAY   3 WEDNESDAY   4 THURSDAY

1 MONDAY	2 TUESDAY	3 WEDNESDAY	4 THURSDAY
7	7	7	7
8	8	8	8
9	9	9	9
10	10	10	10
11	11	11	11
12 PM	12 PM	12 PM	12 PM
1	1	1	1
2	2	2	2
3	3	3	3
4	4	4	4
5	5	5	5
6	6	6	6
7	7	7	7
8	8	8	8
9	9	9	9

5 FRIDAY

6 SATURDAY

7 SUNDAY

5 FRIDAY	6 SATURDAY	7 SUNDAY	Notes
7	7	7	
8	8	8	
9	9	9	
10	10	10	
11	11	11	
12 PM	12 PM	12 PM	
1	1	1	
2	2	2	
3	3	3	To-Do
4	4	4	○
			○
5	5	5	○
			○
6	6	6	○
			○
7	7	7	○
			○
8	8	8	○
			○
9	9	9	○
			○
			○
			○

8 MONDAY

9 TUESDAY

10 WEDNESDAY

11 THURSDAY

7	7	7	7
8	8	8	8
9	9	9	9
10	10	10	10
11	11	11	11
12 PM	12 PM	12 PM	12 PM
1	1	1	1
2	2	2	2
3	3	3	3
4	4	4	4
5	5	5	5
6	6	6	6
7	7	7	7
8	8	8	8
9	9	9	9

12 FRIDAY

13 SATURDAY

14 SUNDAY

12 FRIDAY	13 SATURDAY	14 SUNDAY
7	7	7
8	8	8
9	9	9
10	10	10
11	11	11
12 PM	12 PM	12 PM
1	1	1
2	2	2
3	3	3
4	4	4
5	5	5
6	6	6
7	7	7
8	8	8
9	9	9

Notes

To-Do

- ◯
- ◯
- ◯
- ◯
- ◯
- ◯
- ◯
- ◯
- ◯
- ◯
- ◯
- ◯
- ◯
- ◯

15 MONDAY

7

8

9

10

11

12 PM

1

2

3

4

5

6

7

8

9

16 TUESDAY

7

8

9

10

11

12 PM

1

2

3

4

5

6

7

8

9

17 WEDNESDAY

7

8

9

10

11

12 PM

1

2

3

4

5

6

7

8

9

18 THURSDAY

7

8

9

10

11

12 PM

1

2

3

4

5

6

7

8

9

19 FRIDAY

20 SATURDAY

21 SUNDAY

19 FRIDAY	20 SATURDAY	21 SUNDAY
7	7	7
8	8	8
9	9	9
10	10	10
11	11	11
12 PM	12 PM	12 PM
1	1	1
2	2	2
3	3	3
4	4	4
5	5	5
6	6	6
7	7	7
8	8	8
9	9	9

Notes

To-Do

- ○
- ○
- ○
- ○
- ○
- ○
- ○
- ○
- ○
- ○
- ○
- ○
- ○
- ○

22 MONDAY

23 TUESDAY

24 WEDNESDAY

25 THURSDAY

22 MONDAY	23 TUESDAY	24 WEDNESDAY	25 THURSDAY
7	7	7	7
8	8	8	8
9	9	9	9
10	10	10	10
11	11	11	11
12 PM	12 PM	12 PM	12 PM
1	1	1	1
2	2	2	2
3	3	3	3
4	4	4	4
5	5	5	5
6	6	6	6
7	7	7	7
8	8	8	8
9	9	9	9

26 FRIDAY

7

8

9

10

11

12 PM

1

2

3

4

5

6

7

8

9

27 SATURDAY

7

8

9

10

11

12 PM

1

2

3

4

5

6

7

8

9

28 SUNDAY

7

8

9

10

11

12 PM

1

2

3

4

5

6

7

8

9

Notes

To-Do

○
○
○
○
○
○
○
○
○
○
○
○
○
○

1 MONDAY

2 TUESDAY

3 WEDNESDAY

4 THURSDAY

7	7	7	7
8	8	8	8
9	9	9	9
10	10	10	10
11	11	11	11
12 PM	12 PM	12 PM	12 PM
1	1	1	1
2	2	2	2
3	3	3	3
4	4	4	4
5	5	5	5
6	6	6	6
7	7	7	7
8	8	8	8
9	9	9	9

5 FRIDAY

6 SATURDAY

7 SUNDAY

5 FRIDAY	6 SATURDAY	7 SUNDAY
7	7	7
8	8	8
9	9	9
10	10	10
11	11	11
12 PM	12 PM	12 PM
1	1	1
2	2	2
3	3	3
4	4	4
5	5	5
6	6	6
7	7	7
8	8	8
9	9	9

Notes

To-Do

○
○
○
○
○
○
○
○
○
○
○
○
○
○

8 MONDAY

7

8

9

10

11

12 PM

1

2

3

4

5

6

7

8

9

9 TUESDAY

7

8

9

10

11

12 PM

1

2

3

4

5

6

7

8

9

10 WEDNESDAY

7

8

9

10

11

12 PM

1

2

3

4

5

6

7

8

9

11 THURSDAY

7

8

9

10

11

12 PM

1

2

3

4

5

6

7

8

9

12 FRIDAY

13 SATURDAY

14 SUNDAY

7	7	7
8	8	8
9	9	9
10	10	10
11	11	11
12 PM	12 PM	12 PM
1	1	1
2	2	2
3	3	3
4	4	4
5	5	5
6	6	6
7	7	7
8	8	8
9	9	9

Notes

To Do

○
○
○
○
○
○
○
○
○
○
○
○
○
○

15 MONDAY   16 TUESDAY   17 WEDNESDAY   18 THURSDAY

15 MONDAY	16 TUESDAY	17 WEDNESDAY	18 THURSDAY
7	7	7	7
8	8	8	8
9	9	9	9
10	10	10	10
11	11	11	11
12 PM	12 PM	12 PM	12 PM
1	1	1	1
2	2	2	2
3	3	3	3
4	4	4	4
5	5	5	5
6	6	6	6
7	7	7	7
8	8	8	8
9	9	9	9

19 FRIDAY

20 SATURDAY

21 SUNDAY

19 FRIDAY

7

8

9

10

11

12 PM

1

2

3

4

5

6

7

8

9

20 SATURDAY

7

8

9

10

11

12 PM

1

2

3

4

5

6

7

8

9

21 SUNDAY

7

8

9

10

11

12 PM

1

2

3

4

5

6

7

8

9

Notes

To-Do

○
○
○
○
○
○
○
○
○
○
○
○
○
○

22 MONDAY

7

8

9

10

11

12 PM

1

2

3

4

5

6

7

8

9

23 TUESDAY

7

8

9

10

11

12 PM

1

2

3

4

5

6

7

8

9

24 WEDNESDAY

7

8

9

10

11

12 PM

1

2

3

4

5

6

7

8

9

25 THURSDAY

7

8

9

10

11

12 PM

1

2

3

4

5

6

7

8

9

26 FRIDAY

27 SATURDAY

28 SUNDAY

Notes

26 FRIDAY	27 SATURDAY	28 SUNDAY
7	7	7
8	8	8
9	9	9
10	10	10
11	11	11
12 PM	12 PM	12 PM
1	1	1
2	2	2
3	3	3
4	4	4
5	5	5
6	6	6
7	7	7
8	8	8
9	9	9

To-Do

- ○
- ○
- ○
- ○
- ○
- ○
- ○
- ○
- ○
- ○
- ○
- ○
- ○
- ○

29 MONDAY

7	
8	
9	
10	
11	
12 PM	
1	
2	
3	
4	
5	
6	
7	
8	
9	

30 TUESDAY

7	
8	
9	
10	
11	
12 PM	
1	
2	
3	
4	
5	
6	
7	
8	
9	

31 WEDNESDAY

7	
8	
9	
10	
11	
12 PM	
1	
2	
3	
4	
5	
6	
7	
8	
9	

1 THURSDAY

7	
8	
9	
10	
11	
12 PM	
1	
2	
3	
4	
5	
6	
7	
8	
9	

2 FRIDAY

7

8

9

10

11

12 PM

1

2

3

4

5

6

7

8

9

3 SATURDAY

7

8

9

10

11

12 PM

1

2

3

4

5

6

7

8

9

4 SUNDAY

7

8

9

10

11

12 PM

1

2

3

4

5

6

7

8

9

Notes

To-Do

○
○
○
○
○
○
○
○
○
○
○
○
○
○

5 MONDAY

7

8

9

10

11

12 PM

1

2

3

4

5

6

7

8

9

6 TUESDAY

7

8

9

10

11

12 PM

1

2

3

4

5

6

7

8

9

7 WEDNESDAY

7

8

9

10

11

12 PM

1

2

3

4

5

6

7

8

9

8 THURSDAY

7

8

9

10

11

12 PM

1

2

3

4

5

6

7

8

9

9 FRIDAY

10 SATURDAY

11 SUNDAY

9 Friday	10 Saturday	11 Sunday
7	7	7
8	8	8
9	9	9
10	10	10
11	11	11
12 PM	12 PM	12 PM
1	1	1
2	2	2
3	3	3
4	4	4
5	5	5
6	6	6
7	7	7
8	8	8
9	9	9

Notes

To-Do

○
○
○
○
○
○
○
○
○
○
○
○
○
○

12 MONDAY

7

8

9

10

11

12 PM

1

2

3

4

5

6

7

8

9

13 TUESDAY

7

8

9

10

11

12 PM

1

2

3

4

5

6

7

8

9

14 WEDNESDAY

7

8

9

10

11

12 PM

1

2

3

4

5

6

7

8

9

15 THURSDAY

7

8

9

10

11

12 PM

1

2

3

4

5

6

7

8

9

Notes

7

7

7

8

8

8

9

9

9

10

10

10

11

11

11

12 PM

12 PM

12 PM

1

1

1

2

2

2

3

3

3

to-Do

4

4

4
- ○

- ○

5

5

5
- ○

- ○

6

6

6
- ○

- ○

7

7

7
- ○

- ○

8

8

8
- ○

- ○

9

9

9
- ○

- ○

- ○

- ○

19 MONDAY | 20 TUESDAY | 21 WEDNESDAY | 22 THURSDAY

19 MONDAY	20 TUESDAY	21 WEDNESDAY	22 THURSDAY
7	7	7	7
8	8	8	8
9	9	9	9
10	10	10	10
11	11	11	11
12 PM	12 PM	12 PM	12 PM
1	1	1	1
2	2	2	2
3	3	3	3
4	4	4	4
5	5	5	5
6	6	6	6
7	7	7	7
8	8	8	8
9	9	9	9

23 FRIDAY

24 SATURDAY

25 SUNDAY

23 FRIDAY

7

8

9

10

11

12 PM

1

2

3

4

5

6

7

8

9

24 SATURDAY

7

8

9

10

11

12 PM

1

2

3

4

5

6

7

8

9

25 SUNDAY

7

8

9

10

11

12 PM

1

2

3

4

5

6

7

8

9

Notes

To-Do

○
○
○
○
○
○
○
○
○
○
○
○
○
○

26 MONDAY

7

8

9

10

11

12 PM

1

2

3

4

5

6

7

8

9

27 TUESDAY

7

8

9

10

11

12 PM

1

2

3

4

5

6

7

8

9

28 WEDNESDAY

7

8

9

10

11

12 PM

1

2

3

4

5

6

7

8

9

29 THURSDAY

7

8

9

10

11

12 PM

1

2

3

4

5

6

7

8

9

30 FRIDAY   # 1 SATURDAY   # 2 SUNDAY

30 FRIDAY	1 SATURDAY	2 SUNDAY
7	7	7
8	8	8
9	9	9
10	10	10
11	11	11
12 PM	12 PM	12 PM
1	1	1
2	2	2
3	3	3
4	4	4
5	5	5
6	6	6
7	7	7
8	8	8
9	9	9

Notes

To-Do

○
○
○
○
○
○
○
○
○
○
○
○
○
○

3 MONDAY 4 TUESDAY 5 WEDNESDAY 6 THURSDAY

3 MONDAY	4 TUESDAY	5 WEDNESDAY	6 THURSDAY
7	7	7	7
8	8	8	8
9	9	9	9
10	10	10	10
11	11	11	11
12 PM	12 PM	12 PM	12 PM
1	1	1	1
2	2	2	2
3	3	3	3
4	4	4	4
5	5	5	5
6	6	6	6
7	7	7	7
8	8	8	8
9	9	9	9

7 FRIDAY

8 SATURDAY

9 SUNDAY

7	7	7
8	8	8
9	9	9
10	10	10
11	11	11
12 PM	12 PM	12 PM
1	1	1
2	2	2
3	3	3
4	4	4
5	5	5
6	6	6
7	7	7
8	8	8
9	9	9

Notes

To-Do

- ○
- ○
- ○
- ○
- ○
- ○
- ○
- ○
- ○
- ○
- ○
- ○
- ○
- ○

10 MONDAY

7

8

9

10

11

12 PM

1

2

3

4

5

6

7

8

9

11 TUESDAY

7

8

9

10

11

12 PM

1

2

3

4

5

6

7

8

9

12 WEDNESDAY

7

8

9

10

11

12 PM

1

2

3

4

5

6

7

8

9

13 THURSDAY

7

8

9

10

11

12 PM

1

2

3

4

5

6

7

8

9

14 FRIDAY

15 SATURDAY

16 SUNDAY

14 FRIDAY	15 SATURDAY	16 SUNDAY
7	7	7
8	8	8
9	9	9
10	10	10
11	11	11
12 PM	12 PM	12 PM
1	1	1
2	2	2
3	3	3
4	4	4
5	5	5
6	6	6
7	7	7
8	8	8
9	9	9

Notes

To-Do

○
○
○
○
○
○
○
○
○
○
○
○
○
○

17 MONDAY　18 TUESDAY　19 WEDNESDAY　20 THURSDAY

17 MONDAY	18 TUESDAY	19 WEDNESDAY	20 THURSDAY
7	7	7	7
8	8	8	8
9	9	9	9
10	10	10	10
11	11	11	11
12 PM	12 PM	12 PM	12 PM
1	1	1	1
2	2	2	2
3	3	3	3
4	4	4	4
5	5	5	5
6	6	6	6
7	7	7	7
8	8	8	8
9	9	9	9

21 FRIDAY	22 SATURDAY	23 SUNDAY	Notes
7	7	7	
8	8	8	
9	9	9	
10	10	10	
11	11	11	
12 PM	12 PM	12 PM	
1	1	1	
2	2	2	
3	3	3	To Do
4	4	4	○
5	5	5	○ ○
6	6	6	○ ○
7	7	7	○ ○
8	8	8	○ ○
9	9	9	○ ○ ○ ○

24 MONDAY   25 TUESDAY   26 WEDNESDAY   27 THURSDAY

24 MONDAY	25 TUESDAY	26 WEDNESDAY	27 THURSDAY
7	7	7	7
8	8	8	8
9	9	9	9
10	10	10	10
11	11	11	11
12 PM	12 PM	12 PM	12 PM
1	1	1	1
2	2	2	2
3	3	3	3
4	4	4	4
5	5	5	5
6	6	6	6
7	7	7	7
8	8	8	8
9	9	9	9

28 FRIDAY

29 SATURDAY

30 SUNDAY

28 FRIDAY	29 SATURDAY	30 SUNDAY
7	7	7
8	8	8
9	9	9
10	10	10
11	11	11
12 PM	12 PM	12 PM
1	1	1
2	2	2
3	3	3
4	4	4
5	5	5
6	6	6
7	7	7
8	8	8
9	9	9

Notes

to-Do

- ○
- ○
- ○
- ○
- ○
- ○
- ○
- ○
- ○
- ○
- ○
- ○
- ○
- ○

31 MONDAY

1 TUESDAY

2 WEDNESDAY

3 THURSDAY

31 MONDAY	1 TUESDAY	2 WEDNESDAY	3 THURSDAY
7	7	7	7
8	8	8	8
9	9	9	9
10	10	10	10
11	11	11	11
12 PM	12 PM	12 PM	12 PM
1	1	1	1
2	2	2	2
3	3	3	3
4	4	4	4
5	5	5	5
6	6	6	6
7	7	7	7
8	8	8	8
9	9	9	9

4 FRIDAY

5 SATURDAY

6 SUNDAY

Notes

7

7

7

8

8

8

9

9

9

10

10

10

11

11

11

12 PM

12 PM

12 PM

1

1

1

2

2

2

3

3

3

To-Do

4

4

4

○
○

5

5

5

○
○

6

6

6

○
○

7

7

7

○
○

8

8

8

○
○

9

9

9

○
○
○
○

7 MONDAY

7

8

9

10

11

12 PM

1

2

3

4

5

6

7

8

9

8 TUESDAY

7

8

9

10

11

12 PM

1

2

3

4

5

6

7

8

9

9 WEDNESDAY

7

8

9

10

11

12 PM

1

2

3

4

5

6

7

8

9

10 THURSDAY

7

8

9

10

11

12 PM

1

2

3

4

5

6

7

8

9

11 FRIDAY

12 SATURDAY

13 SUNDAY

Notes

7

8

9

10

11

12 PM

1

2

3

4

5

6

7

8

9

to-Do

○
○
○
○
○
○
○
○
○
○
○
○
○
○

14 MONDAY

7

8

9

10

11

12 PM

1

2

3

4

5

6

7

8

9

15 TUESDAY

7

8

9

10

11

12 PM

1

2

3

4

5

6

7

8

9

16 WEDNESDAY

7

8

9

10

11

12 PM

1

2

3

4

5

6

7

8

9

17 THURSDAY

7

8

9

10

11

12 PM

1

2

3

4

5

6

7

8

9

18 FRIDAY   19 SATURDAY   20 SUNDAY

18 FRIDAY	19 SATURDAY	20 SUNDAY
7	7	7
8	8	8
9	9	9
10	10	10
11	11	11
12 PM	12 PM	12 PM
1	1	1
2	2	2
3	3	3
4	4	4
5	5	5
6	6	6
7	7	7
8	8	8
9	9	9

Notes

To-Do

○
○
○
○
○
○
○
○
○
○
○
○
○
○

21 MONDAY

7

8

9

10

11

12 PM

1

2

3

4

5

6

7

8

9

22 TUESDAY

7

8

9

10

11

12 PM

1

2

3

4

5

6

7

8

9

23 WEDNESDAY

7

8

9

10

11

12 PM

1

2

3

4

5

6

7

8

9

24 THURSDAY

7

8

9

10

11

12 PM

1

2

3

4

5

6

7

8

9

25 FRIDAY

26 SATURDAY

27 SUNDAY

Notes

7

8

9

10

11

12 PM

1

2

3

4

5

6

7

8

9

to-Do

○
○
○
○
○
○
○
○
○
○
○
○
○
○

28 MONDAY

7

8

9

10

11

12 PM

1

2

3

4

5

6

7

8

9

29 TUESDAY

7

8

9

10

11

12 PM

1

2

3

4

5

6

7

8

9

30 WEDNESDAY

7

8

9

10

11

12 PM

1

2

3

4

5

6

7

8

9

1 THURSDAY

7

8

9

10

11

12 PM

1

2

3

4

5

6

7

8

9

2 FRIDAY

3 SATURDAY

4 SUNDAY

2 FRIDAY	3 SATURDAY	4 SUNDAY
7	7	7
8	8	8
9	9	9
10	10	10
11	11	11
12 PM	12 PM	12 PM
1	1	1
2	2	2
3	3	3
4	4	4
5	5	5
6	6	6
7	7	7
8	8	8
9	9	9

Notes

To-Do

○
○
○
○
○
○
○
○
○
○
○
○
○
○

5 MONDAY

7

8

9

10

11

12 PM

1

2

3

4

5

6

7

8

9

6 TUESDAY

7

8

9

10

11

12 PM

1

2

3

4

5

6

7

8

9

7 WEDNESDAY

7

8

9

10

11

12 PM

1

2

3

4

5

6

7

8

9

8 THURSDAY

7

8

9

10

11

12 PM

1

2

3

4

5

6

7

8

9

9 FRIDAY
10 SATURDAY
11 SUNDAY

9 FRIDAY	10 SATURDAY	11 SUNDAY
7	7	7
8	8	8
9	9	9
10	10	10
11	11	11
12 PM	12 PM	12 PM
1	1	1
2	2	2
3	3	3
4	4	4
5	5	5
6	6	6
7	7	7
8	8	8
9	9	9

Notes

To Do

○
○
○
○
○
○
○
○
○
○
○
○
○
○

12 MONDAY

7

8

9

10

11

12 PM

1

2

3

4

5

6

7

8

9

13 TUESDAY

7

8

9

10

11

12 PM

1

2

3

4

5

6

7

8

9

14 WEDNESDAY

7

8

9

10

11

12 PM

1

2

3

4

5

6

7

8

9

15 THURSDAY

7

8

9

10

11

12 PM

1

2

3

4

5

6

7

8

9

16 FRIDAY

7

8

9

10

11

12 PM

1

2

3

4

5

6

7

8

9

17 SATURDAY

7

8

9

10

11

12 PM

1

2

3

4

5

6

7

8

9

18 SUNDAY

7

8

9

10

11

12 PM

1

2

3

4

5

6

7

8

9

Notes

To-Do

○
○
○
○
○
○
○
○
○
○
○
○
○
○

19 MONDAY	**20** TUESDAY	**21** WEDNESDAY	**22** THURSDAY
7	7	7	7
8	8	8	8
9	9	9	9
10	10	10	10
11	11	11	11
12 PM	12 PM	12 PM	12 PM
1	1	1	1
2	2	2	2
3	3	3	3
4	4	4	4
5	5	5	5
6	6	6	6
7	7	7	7
8	8	8	8
9	9	9	9

23 FRIDAY

7

8

9

10

11

12 PM

1

2

3

4

5

6

7

8

9

24 SATURDAY

7

8

9

10

11

12 PM

1

2

3

4

5

6

7

8

9

25 SUNDAY

7

8

9

10

11

12 PM

1

2

3

4

5

6

7

8

9

Notes

To-Do

○
○
○
○
○
○
○
○
○
○
○
○
○
○

26 MONDAY

7
8
9
10
11
12 PM
1
2
3
4
5
6
7
8
9

27 TUESDAY

7
8
9
10
11
12 PM
1
2
3
4
5
6
7
8
9

28 WEDNESDAY

7
8
9
10
11
12 PM
1
2
3
4
5
6
7
8
9

29 THURSDAY

7
8
9
10
11
12 PM
1
2
3
4
5
6
7
8
9

30 FRIDAY

31 SATURDAY

1 SUNDAY

30 FRIDAY	31 SATURDAY	1 SUNDAY
7	7	7
8	8	8
9	9	9
10	10	10
11	11	11
12 PM	12 PM	12 PM
1	1	1
2	2	2
3	3	3
4	4	4
5	5	5
6	6	6
7	7	7
8	8	8
9	9	9

Notes

To Do

- ○
- ○
- ○
- ○
- ○
- ○
- ○
- ○
- ○
- ○
- ○
- ○
- ○
- ○

2 MONDAY

7

8

9

10

11

12 PM

1

2

3

4

5

6

7

8

9

3 TUESDAY

7

8

9

10

11

12 PM

1

2

3

4

5

6

7

8

9

4 WEDNESDAY

7

8

9

10

11

12 PM

1

2

3

4

5

6

7

8

9

5 THURSDAY

7

8

9

10

11

12 PM

1

2

3

4

5

6

7

8

9

6 FRIDAY

7 SATURDAY

8 SUNDAY

Notes

6 FRIDAY	7 SATURDAY	8 SUNDAY
7	7	7
8	8	8
9	9	9
10	10	10
11	11	11
12 PM	12 PM	12 PM
1	1	1
2	2	2
3	3	3
4	4	4
5	5	5
6	6	6
7	7	7
8	8	8
9	9	9

To-Do

○
○
○
○
○
○
○
○
○
○
○
○
○
○

9 MONDAY   10 TUESDAY   11 WEDNESDAY   12 THURSDAY

7	7	7	7
8	8	8	8
9	9	9	9
10	10	10	10
11	11	11	11
12 PM	12 PM	12 PM	12 PM
1	1	1	1
2	2	2	2
3	3	3	3
4	4	4	4
5	5	5	5
6	6	6	6
7	7	7	7
8	8	8	8
9	9	9	9

13 FRIDAY	14 SATURDAY	15 SUNDAY	Notes
7	7	7	
8	8	8	
9	9	9	
10	10	10	
11	11	11	
12 PM	12 PM	12 PM	
1	1	1	
2	2	2	
3	3	3	To Do
4	4	4	○
5	5	5	○ ○
6	6	6	○ ○
7	7	7	○ ○
8	8	8	○ ○
9	9	9	○ ○ ○ ○ ○

16 MONDAY

7

8

9

10

11

12 PM

1

2

3

4

5

6

7

8

9

17 TUESDAY

7

8

9

10

11

12 PM

1

2

3

4

5

6

7

8

9

18 WEDNESDAY

7

8

9

10

11

12 PM

1

2

3

4

5

6

7

8

9

19 THURSDAY

7

8

9

10

11

12 PM

1

2

3

4

5

6

7

8

9

20 FRIDAY

21 SATURDAY

22 SUNDAY

20 FRIDAY	21 SATURDAY	22 SUNDAY
7	7	7
8	8	8
9	9	9
10	10	10
11	11	11
12 PM	12 PM	12 PM
1	1	1
2	2	2
3	3	3
4	4	4
5	5	5
6	6	6
7	7	7
8	8	8
9	9	9

Notes

To-Do

○
○
○
○
○
○
○
○
○
○
○
○
○
○

23 MONDAY	**24** TUESDAY	**25** WEDNESDAY	**26** THURSDAY
7	7	7	7
8	8	8	8
9	9	9	9
10	10	10	10
11	11	11	11
12 PM	12 PM	12 PM	12 PM
1	1	1	1
2	2	2	2
3	3	3	3
4	4	4	4
5	5	5	5
6	6	6	6
7	7	7	7
8	8	8	8
9	9	9	9

27 FRIDAY

28 SATURDAY

29 SUNDAY

27 FRIDAY	28 SATURDAY	29 SUNDAY
7	7	7
8	8	8
9	9	9
10	10	10
11	11	11
12 PM	12 PM	12 PM
1	1	1
2	2	2
3	3	3
4	4	4
5	5	5
6	6	6
7	7	7
8	8	8
9	9	9

Notes

To-Do

- ○
- ○
- ○
- ○
- ○
- ○
- ○
- ○
- ○
- ○
- ○
- ○
- ○
- ○

30 MONDAY 31 TUESDAY 1 WEDNESDAY 2 THURSDAY

30 MONDAY	31 TUESDAY	1 WEDNESDAY	2 THURSDAY
7	7	7	7
8	8	8	8
9	9	9	9
10	10	10	10
11	11	11	11
12 PM	12 PM	12 PM	12 PM
1	1	1	1
2	2	2	2
3	3	3	3
4	4	4	4
5	5	5	5
6	6	6	6
7	7	7	7
8	8	8	8
9	9	9	9

3 FRIDAY

7

8

9

10

11

12 PM

1

2

3

4

5

6

7

8

9

4 SATURDAY

7

8

9

10

11

12 PM

1

2

3

4

5

6

7

8

9

5 SUNDAY

7

8

9

10

11

12 PM

1

2

3

4

5

6

7

8

9

Notes

To-Do

○
○
○
○
○
○
○
○
○
○
○
○
○
○

6 MONDAY   7 TUESDAY   8 WEDNESDAY   9 THURSDAY

7	7	7	7
8	8	8	8
9	9	9	9
10	10	10	10
11	11	11	11
12 PM	12 PM	12 PM	12 PM
1	1	1	1
2	2	2	2
3	3	3	3
4	4	4	4
5	5	5	5
6	6	6	6
7	7	7	7
8	8	8	8
9	9	9	9

10 FRIDAY

11 SATURDAY

12 SUNDAY

10 FRIDAY	11 SATURDAY	12 SUNDAY
7	7	7
8	8	8
9	9	9
10	10	10
11	11	11
12 PM	12 PM	12 PM
1	1	1
2	2	2
3	3	3
4	4	4
5	5	5
6	6	6
7	7	7
8	8	8
9	9	9

Notes

To Do

- ○
- ○
- ○
- ○
- ○
- ○
- ○
- ○
- ○
- ○
- ○
- ○
- ○
- ○

13 MONDAY

14 TUESDAY

15 WEDNESDAY

16 THURSDAY

13 MONDAY	14 TUESDAY	15 WEDNESDAY	16 THURSDAY
7	7	7	7
8	8	8	8
9	9	9	9
10	10	10	10
11	11	11	11
12 PM	12 PM	12 PM	12 PM
1	1	1	1
2	2	2	2
3	3	3	3
4	4	4	4
5	5	5	5
6	6	6	6
7	7	7	7
8	8	8	8
9	9	9	9

17 FRIDAY

18 SATURDAY

19 SUNDAY

Notes

17 FRIDAY	18 SATURDAY	19 SUNDAY
7	7	7
8	8	8
9	9	9
10	10	10
11	11	11
12 PM	12 PM	12 PM
1	1	1
2	2	2
3	3	3
4	4	4
5	5	5
6	6	6
7	7	7
8	8	8
9	9	9

To-Do

- ○
- ○
- ○
- ○
- ○
- ○
- ○
- ○
- ○
- ○
- ○
- ○
- ○
- ○

20 MONDAY | 21 TUESDAY | 22 WEDNESDAY | 23 THURSDAY

20 MONDAY	21 TUESDAY	22 WEDNESDAY	23 THURSDAY
7	7	7	7
8	8	8	8
9	9	9	9
10	10	10	10
11	11	11	11
12 PM	12 PM	12 PM	12 PM
1	1	1	1
2	2	2	2
3	3	3	3
4	4	4	4
5	5	5	5
6	6	6	6
7	7	7	7
8	8	8	8
9	9	9	9

24 FRIDAY

7

8

9

10

11

12 PM

1

2

3

4

5

6

7

8

9

25 SATURDAY

7

8

9

10

11

12 PM

1

2

3

4

5

6

7

8

9

26 SUNDAY

7

8

9

10

11

12 PM

1

2

3

4

5

6

7

8

9

Notes

To-Do

○
○
○
○
○
○
○
○
○
○
○
○
○
○

27 MONDAY

7

8

9

10

11

12 PM

1

2

3

4

5

6

7

8

9

28 TUESDAY

7

8

9

10

11

12 PM

1

2

3

4

5

6

7

8

9

29 WEDNESDAY

7

8

9

10

11

12 PM

1

2

3

4

5

6

7

8

9

30 THURSDAY

7

8

9

10

11

12 PM

1

2

3

4

5

6

7

8

9

1 FRIDAY

2 SATURDAY

3 SUNDAY

7	7	7
8	8	8
9	9	9
10	10	10
11	11	11
12 PM	12 PM	12 PM
1	1	1
2	2	2
3	3	3
4	4	4
5	5	5
6	6	6
7	7	7
8	8	8
9	9	9

Notes

To-Do

○
○
○
○
○
○
○
○
○
○
○
○
○
○

4 MONDAY 5 TUESDAY 6 WEDNESDAY 7 THURSDAY

7	7	7	7
8	8	8	8
9	9	9	9
10	10	10	10
11	11	11	11
12 PM	12 PM	12 PM	12 PM
1	1	1	1
2	2	2	2
3	3	3	3
4	4	4	4
5	5	5	5
6	6	6	6
7	7	7	7
8	8	8	8
9	9	9	9

8 FRIDAY

9 SATURDAY

10 SUNDAY

Notes

7	7	7
8	8	8
9	9	9
10	10	10
11	11	11
12 PM	12 PM	12 PM
1	1	1
2	2	2
3	3	3
4	4	4
5	5	5
6	6	6
7	7	7
8	8	8
9	9	9

To-Do

○
○
○
○
○
○
○
○
○
○
○
○
○
○

11 MONDAY

7

8

9

10

11

12 PM

1

2

3

4

5

6

7

8

9

12 TUESDAY

7

8

9

10

11

12 PM

1

2

3

4

5

6

7

8

9

13 WEDNESDAY

7

8

9

10

11

12 PM

1

2

3

4

5

6

7

8

9

14 THURSDAY

7

8

9

10

11

12 PM

1

2

3

4

5

6

7

8

9

15 FRIDAY   16 SATURDAY   17 SUNDAY

15 FRIDAY	16 SATURDAY	17 SUNDAY
7	7	7
8	8	8
9	9	9
10	10	10
11	11	11
12 PM	12 PM	12 PM
1	1	1
2	2	2
3	3	3
4	4	4
5	5	5
6	6	6
7	7	7
8	8	8
9	9	9

Notes

To-Do

○
○
○
○
○
○
○
○
○
○
○
○
○
○

18 MONDAY	**19** TUESDAY	**20** WEDNESDAY	**21** THURSDAY
7	7	7	7
8	8	8	8
9	9	9	9
10	10	10	10
11	11	11	11
12 PM	12 PM	12 PM	12 PM
1	1	1	1
2	2	2	2
3	3	3	3
4	4	4	4
5	5	5	5
6	6	6	6
7	7	7	7
8	8	8	8
9	9	9	9

22 FRIDAY

23 SATURDAY

24 SUNDAY

22 FRIDAY	23 SATURDAY	24 SUNDAY
7	7	7
8	8	8
9	9	9
10	10	10
11	11	11
12 PM	12 PM	12 PM
1	1	1
2	2	2
3	3	3
4	4	4
5	5	5
6	6	6
7	7	7
8	8	8
9	9	9

Notes

To-Do

- ○
- ○
- ○
- ○
- ○
- ○
- ○
- ○
- ○
- ○
- ○
- ○
- ○
- ○

25 MONDAY

7

8

9

10

11

12 PM

1

2

3

4

5

6

7

8

9

26 TUESDAY

7

8

9

10

11

12 PM

1

2

3

4

5

6

7

8

9

27 WEDNESDAY

7

8

9

10

11

12 PM

1

2

3

4

5

6

7

8

9

28 THURSDAY

7

8

9

10

11

12 PM

1

2

3

4

5

6

7

8

9

29 FRIDAY	30 SATURDAY	31 SUNDAY	Notes
7	7	7	
8	8	8	
9	9	9	
10	10	10	
11	11	11	
12 PM	12 PM	12 PM	
1	1	1	
2	2	2	
3	3	3	To-Do
4	4	4	○
5	5	5	○
6	6	6	○
7	7	7	○
8	8	8	○
9	9	9	○

1 MONDAY

7

8

9

10

11

12 PM

1

2

3

4

5

6

7

8

9

2 TUESDAY

7

8

9

10

11

12 PM

1

2

3

4

5

6

7

8

9

3 WEDNESDAY

7

8

9

10

11

12 PM

1

2

3

4

5

6

7

8

9

4 THURSDAY

7

8

9

10

11

12 PM

1

2

3

4

5

6

7

8

9

5 FRIDAY

6 SATURDAY

7 SUNDAY

5 FRIDAY	6 SATURDAY	7 SUNDAY
7	7	7
8	8	8
9	9	9
10	10	10
11	11	11
12 PM	12 PM	12 PM
1	1	1
2	2	2
3	3	3
4	4	4
5	5	5
6	6	6
7	7	7
8	8	8
9	9	9

Notes

To Do

○
○
○
○
○
○
○
○
○
○
○
○
○
○

8 MONDAY

7

8

9

10

11

12 PM

1

2

3

4

5

6

7

8

9

9 TUESDAY

7

8

9

10

11

12 PM

1

2

3

4

5

6

7

8

9

10 WEDNESDAY

7

8

9

10

11

12 PM

1

2

3

4

5

6

7

8

9

11 THURSDAY

7

8

9

10

11

12 PM

1

2

3

4

5

6

7

8

9

12 FRIDAY

13 SATURDAY

14 SUNDAY

12 FRIDAY	13 SATURDAY	14 SUNDAY
7	7	7
8	8	8
9	9	9
10	10	10
11	11	11
12 PM	12 PM	12 PM
1	1	1
2	2	2
3	3	3
4	4	4
5	5	5
6	6	6
7	7	7
8	8	8
9	9	9

Notes

To-Do

○
○
○
○
○
○
○
○
○
○
○
○
○
○

15 MONDAY   16 TUESDAY   17 WEDNESDAY   18 THURSDAY

7	7	7	7
8	8	8	8
9	9	9	9
10	10	10	10
11	11	11	11
12 PM	12 PM	12 PM	12 PM
1	1	1	1
2	2	2	2
3	3	3	3
4	4	4	4
5	5	5	5
6	6	6	6
7	7	7	7
8	8	8	8
9	9	9	9

19 FRIDAY

7

8

9

10

11

12 PM

1

2

3

4

5

6

7

8

9

20 SATURDAY

7

8

9

10

11

12 PM

1

2

3

4

5

6

7

8

9

21 SUNDAY

7

8

9

10

11

12 PM

1

2

3

4

5

6

7

8

9

Notes

To-Do

○
○
○
○
○
○
○
○
○
○
○
○
○
○

22 MONDAY

7

8

9

10

11

12 PM

1

2

3

4

5

6

7

8

9

23 TUESDAY

7

8

9

10

11

12 PM

1

2

3

4

5

6

7

8

9

24 WEDNESDAY

7

8

9

10

11

12 PM

1

2

3

4

5

6

7

8

9

25 THURSDAY

7

8

9

10

11

12 PM

1

2

3

4

5

6

7

8

9

26 FRIDAY	27 SATURDAY	28 SUNDAY	Notes
7	7	7	
8	8	8	
9	9	9	
10	10	10	
11	11	11	
12 PM	12 PM	12 PM	
1	1	1	
2	2	2	
3	3	3	To Do
4	4	4	○
			○
5	5	5	○
			○
6	6	6	○
			○
7	7	7	○
			○
8	8	8	○
			○
9	9	9	○
			○
			○
			○

29 MONDAY   30 TUESDAY   1 WEDNESDAY   2 THURSDAY

29 MONDAY	30 TUESDAY	1 WEDNESDAY	2 THURSDAY
7	7	7	7
8	8	8	8
9	9	9	9
10	10	10	10
11	11	11	11
12 PM	12 PM	12 PM	12 PM
1	1	1	1
2	2	2	2
3	3	3	3
4	4	4	4
5	5	5	5
6	6	6	6
7	7	7	7
8	8	8	8
9	9	9	9

3 FRIDAY

7

8

9

10

11

12 PM

1

2

3

4

5

6

7

8

9

4 SATURDAY

7

8

9

10

11

12 PM

1

2

3

4

5

6

7

8

9

5 SUNDAY

7

8

9

10

11

12 PM

1

2

3

4

5

6

7

8

9

Notes

_To-Do_

○
○
○
○
○
○
○
○
○
○
○
○
○
○

6 MONDAY	**7** TUESDAY	**8** WEDNESDAY	**9** THURSDAY
7	7	7	7
8	8	8	8
9	9	9	9
10	10	10	10
11	11	11	11
12 PM	12 PM	12 PM	12 PM
1	1	1	1
2	2	2	2
3	3	3	3
4	4	4	4
5	5	5	5
6	6	6	6
7	7	7	7
8	8	8	8
9	9	9	9

10 FRIDAY | **11** SATURDAY | **12** SUNDAY

10 FRIDAY	11 SATURDAY	12 SUNDAY
7	7	7
8	8	8
9	9	9
10	10	10
11	11	11
12 PM	12 PM	12 PM
1	1	1
2	2	2
3	3	3
4	4	4
5	5	5
6	6	6
7	7	7
8	8	8
9	9	9

Notes

To-Do

- ○
- ○
- ○
- ○
- ○
- ○
- ○
- ○
- ○
- ○
- ○
- ○
- ○
- ○

13 MONDAY

7

8

9

10

11

12 PM

1

2

3

4

5

6

7

8

9

14 TUESDAY

7

8

9

10

11

12 PM

1

2

3

4

5

6

7

8

9

15 WEDNESDAY

7

8

9

10

11

12 PM

1

2

3

4

5

6

7

8

9

16 THURSDAY

7

8

9

10

11

12 PM

1

2

3

4

5

6

7

8

9

17 FRIDAY

18 SATURDAY

19 SUNDAY

17 FRIDAY	18 SATURDAY	19 SUNDAY
7	7	7
8	8	8
9	9	9
10	10	10
11	11	11
12 PM	12 PM	12 PM
1	1	1
2	2	2
3	3	3
4	4	4
5	5	5
6	6	6
7	7	7
8	8	8
9	9	9

Notes

to-Do

○
○
○
○
○
○
○
○
○
○
○
○
○
○

20 MONDAY	**21** TUESDAY	**22** WEDNESDAY	**23** THURSDAY
7	7	7	7
8	8	8	8
9	9	9	9
10	10	10	10
11	11	11	11
12 PM	12 PM	12 PM	12 PM
1	1	1	1
2	2	2	2
3	3	3	3
4	4	4	4
5	5	5	5
6	6	6	6
7	7	7	7
8	8	8	8
9	9	9	9

24 FRIDAY

25 SATURDAY

26 SUNDAY

Notes

24 FRIDAY	25 SATURDAY	26 SUNDAY
7	7	7
8	8	8
9	9	9
10	10	10
11	11	11
12 PM	12 PM	12 PM
1	1	1
2	2	2
3	3	3
4	4	4
5	5	5
6	6	6
7	7	7
8	8	8
9	9	9

To-Do

○
○
○
○
○
○
○
○
○
○
○
○
○
○

27 MONDAY

28 TUESDAY

29 WEDNESDAY

30 THURSDAY

27 MONDAY	28 TUESDAY	29 WEDNESDAY	30 THURSDAY
7	7	7	7
8	8	8	8
9	9	9	9
10	10	10	10
11	11	11	11
12 PM	12 PM	12 PM	12 PM
1	1	1	1
2	2	2	2
3	3	3	3
4	4	4	4
5	5	5	5
6	6	6	6
7	7	7	7
8	8	8	8
9	9	9	9

31 FRIDAY

1 SATURDAY

2 SUNDAY

31 FRIDAY	1 SATURDAY	2 SUNDAY
7	7	7
8	8	8
9	9	9
10	10	10
11	11	11
12 PM	12 PM	12 PM
1	1	1
2	2	2
3	3	3
4	4	4
5	5	5
6	6	6
7	7	7
8	8	8
9	9	9

Notes

To-Do

- ○
- ○
- ○
- ○
- ○
- ○
- ○
- ○
- ○
- ○
- ○
- ○
- ○
- ○

MONDAY	TUESDAY	WEDNESDAY	THURSDAY
29	30	1	2
6	7	8	9
13	14	15	16
20	21	22	23
27	28	29	30

FRIDAY	SATURDAY	SUNDAY	
3	4	5	
10	11	12	
17	18	19	
24	25	26	
31	1	2	

MONDAY	TUESDAY	WEDNESDAY	THURSDAY
27	28	29	30
3	4	5	6
10	11	12	13
17	18	19	20
24	25	26	27
31			

FRIDAY	SATURDAY	SUNDAY
31	1	2
7	8	9
14	15	16
21	22	23
28	29	30

MONDAY	TUESDAY	WEDNESDAY	THURSDAY
31	1	2	3
7	8	9	10
14	15	16	17
21	22	23	24
28	29	30	1

FRIDAY	SATURDAY	SUNDAY
4	5	6
11	12	13
18	19	20
25	26	27
2	3	4

MONDAY	TUESDAY	WEDNESDAY	THURSDAY
28	29	30	1
5	6	7	8
12	13	14	15
19	20	21	22
26	27	28	29

FRIDAY	SATURDAY	SUNDAY
2	3	4
9	10	11
16	17	18
23	24	25
30	31	

MONDAY	TUESDAY	WEDNESDAY	THURSDAY
26	27	28	29
2	3	4	5
9	10	11	12
16	17	18	19
23 30	24	25	26

FRIDAY	SATURDAY	SUNDAY
30	31	1
6	7	8
13	14	15
20	21	22
27	28	29

MONDAY	TUESDAY	WEDNESDAY	THURSDAY
30	1	2	3
7	8	9	10
14	15	16	17
21	22	23	24
28	29	30	31

FRIDAY	SATURDAY	SUNDAY
4	5	6
11	12	13
18	19	20
25	26	27
1	2	3

MONDAY	TUESDAY	WEDNESDAY	THURSDAY
28	29	30	31
4	5	6	7
11	12	13	14
18	19	20	21
25	26	27	28

JANUARY 2021

FRIDAY	SATURDAY	SUNDAY
1	2	3
8	9	10
15	16	17
22	23	24
29	30	31

MONDAY	TUESDAY	WEDNESDAY	THURSDAY
1	2	3	4
8	9	10	11
15	16	17	18
22	23	24	25
1	2	3	4

FRIDAY	SATURDAY	SUNDAY
5	6	7
12	13	14
19	20	21
26	27	28
5	6	7

MONDAY	TUESDAY	WEDNESDAY	THURSDAY
1	2	3	4
8	9	10	11
15	16	17	18
22	23	24	25
29	30	31	1

FRIDAY	SATURDAY	SUNDAY
5	6	7
12	13	14
19	20	21
26	27	28
2	3	4

MONDAY	TUESDAY	WEDNESDAY	THURSDAY
29	30	31	1
5	6	7	8
12	13	14	15
19	20	21	22
26	27	28	29

FRIDAY	SATURDAY	SUNDAY
2	3	4
9	10	11
16	17	18
23	24	25
30	1	2

MONDAY	TUESDAY	WEDNESDAY	THURSDAY
26	27	28	29
3	4	5	6
10	11	12	13
17	18	19	20
24	25	26	27
31			

FRIDAY	SATURDAY	SUNDAY
30	1	2
7	8	9
14	15	16
21	22	23
28	29	30

MONDAY	TUESDAY	WEDNESDAY	THURSDAY
31	1	2	3
7	8	9	10
14	15	16	17
21	22	23	24
28	29	30	1

FRIDAY	SATURDAY	SUNDAY
4	5	6
11	12	13
18	19	20
25	26	27
2	3	4

MONDAY	TUESDAY	WEDNESDAY	THURSDAY
28	29	30	1
5	6	7	8
12	13	14	15
19	20	21	22
26	27	28	29

FRIDAY	SATURDAY	SUNDAY
2	3	4
9	10	11
16	17	18
23	24	25
30	31	1

MONDAY	TUESDAY	WEDNESDAY	THURSDAY
26	27	28	29
2	3	4	5
9	10	11	12
16	17	18	19
23	24	25	26
30	31		

FRIDAY	SATURDAY	SUNDAY
30	31	1
6	7	8
13	14	15
20	21	22
27	28	29

MONDAY	TUESDAY	WEDNESDAY	THURSDAY
30	31	1	2
6	7	8	9
13	14	15	16
20	21	22	23
27	28	29	30

FRIDAY	SATURDAY	SUNDAY
3	4	5
10	11	12
17	18	19
24	25	26
1	2	3

MONDAY	TUESDAY	WEDNESDAY	THURSDAY
27	28	29	30
4	5	6	7
11	12	13	14
18	19	20	21
25	26	27	28

FRIDAY	SATURDAY	SUNDAY
1	2	3
8	9	10
15	16	17
22	23	24
29	30	31

MONDAY	TUESDAY	WEDNESDAY	THURSDAY
1	2	3	4
8	9	10	11
15	16	17	18
22	23	24	25
29	30	1	2

FRIDAY	SATURDAY	SUNDAY
5	6	7
12	13	14
19	20	21
26	27	28
3	4	5

MONDAY	TUESDAY	WEDNESDAY	THURSDAY
29	30	1	2
6	7	8	9
13	14	15	16
20	21	22	23
27	28	29	30

FRIDAY	SATURDAY	SUNDAY
3	4	5
10	11	12
17	18	19
24	25	26
31	1	2

🕐	MON	TUE	WED	THU	FRI	SAT	SUN

_____

_____

_____

_____

_____

_____

WEEKLY SCHEDULE

🕐	MON	TUE	WED	THU	FRI	SAT	SUN

Date:	Subject:
Participants:	

Notes

Date:	Subject:
Participants:	

Notes

MEETING NOTES

Date:	Subject:
Participants:	

Notes

Date:	Subject:
Participants:	

Notes

Date:	Subject:
Participants:	

Notes

Date:	Subject:
Participants:	

Notes

MEETING NOTES

Date:	Subject:
Participants:	

Notes

Date:	Subject:
Participants:	

Notes

Date:	Subject:
Participants:	

Notes

Date:	Subject:
Participants:	

Notes

MEETING NOTES

Date:	Subject:
Participants:	

Notes

Date:	Subject:
Participants:	

Notes

Date:	Subject:
Participants:	

Notes

Date:	Subject:
Participants:	

Notes

MEETING NOTES

Date:	Subject:
Participants:	

Notes

Date:	Subject:
Participants:	

Notes

👤 _____
📞 _____
@ _____

👤 _____
📞 _____
@ _____

👤 _____
📞 _____
@ _____

👤 _____
📞 _____
@ _____

👤 _____
📞 _____
@ _____

👤 _____
📞 _____
@ _____

👤 _____
📞 _____
@ _____

👤 _____
📞 _____
@ _____

CONTACTS

CPSIA information can be obtained
at www.ICGtesting.com
Printed in the USA
BVHW010339151020
591043BV00003B/88